ROME TRAVEL GUIDE

HUNGRY PASSPORT

How to use this guide?

SECTIONS ARE DIVIDED BY COLORS

SECTION I

Things to know before you go

Packed with practical info from how to get from the airport to Rome, how to get around the city, the best time to visit, the best apps to use, which tours to take, etc.

SECTION II & III

Top 10 attractions & 10 additional ones

The absolute must-see 10 attractions, especially if you are visiting for the first time. If you have more time, find additional impressive landmarks and experiences.

SECTION IV

Itineraries, Day trips, Things to do when...

If you don't have the time to plan your own itinerary, you'll find things to do if it's raining, in the winter, in the evening, best day trips, and more.

THIS GUIDE IS INTERACTIVE

Scan the QR code

- Maps
- Tickets
- Apps
- Info

TABLE OF CONTENTS

Section 1
Things to Know Before You Go — 5

Section 2
Top 10 Things to Do — 27

Section 3
10 Additional Things to Do — 55

Section 4
Itineraries, Day Trips, etc. — 79

Main MAP

This map includes:
Top 20 Rome, Best city views, etc.

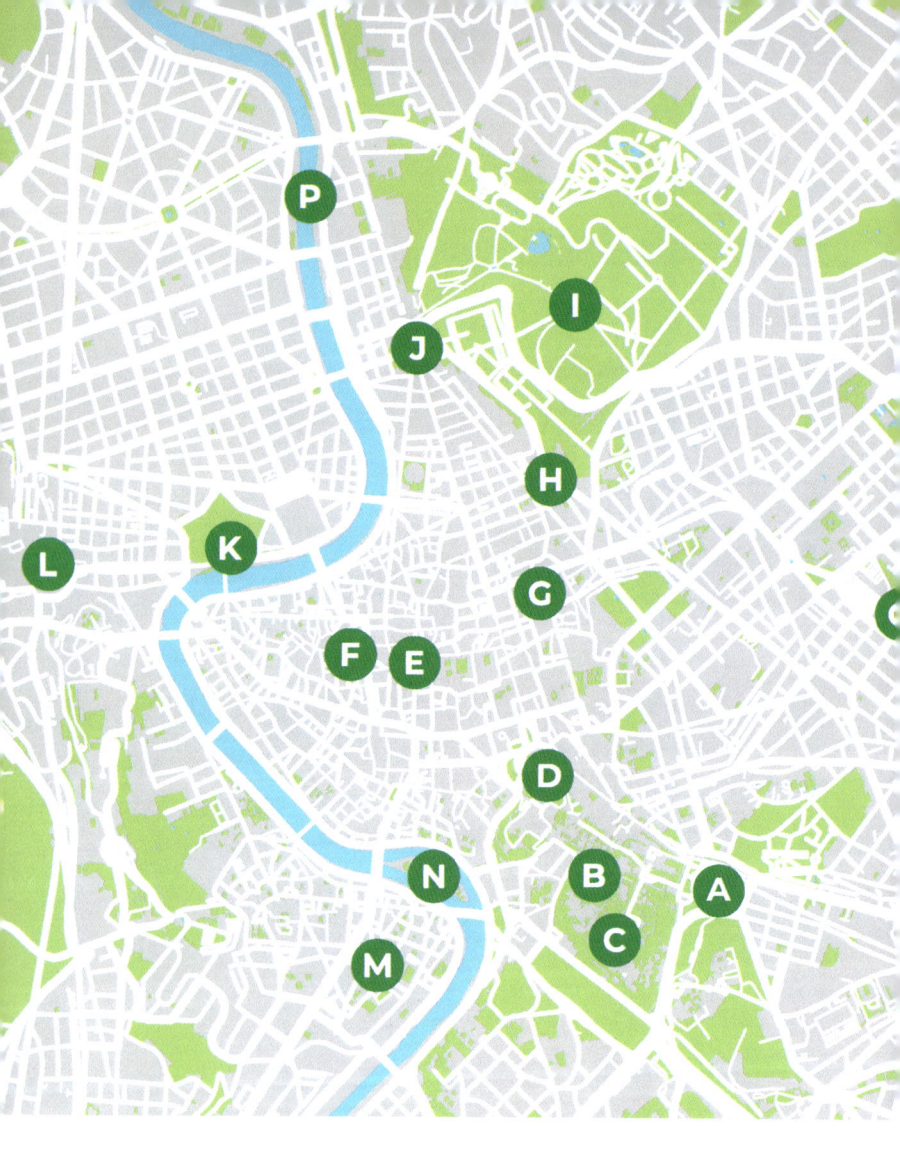

- Ⓐ Colosseum
- Ⓑ Roman Forum
- Ⓒ Capitoline Hill
- Ⓓ Altare della Patria
- Ⓔ Pantheon
- Ⓕ Piazza Navona
- Ⓖ Trevi Fountain
- Ⓗ Spanish Steps
- Ⓘ Villa Borghese
- Ⓙ Piazza del Popolo
- Ⓚ Castel Sant'Angelo
- Ⓛ Vatican City
- Ⓜ Trastevere
- Ⓝ Tiber Island
- Ⓞ Train Station
- Ⓟ River Tiber

Section 1

Things to Know Before You Go to Rome

This section includes:

I. General Info	6
II. Money	8
III. Weather & Climate	9
IV. Transportation	10
V. Accommodation	16
VI. Food & Drinks	17
VII. Good to Know	18
VIII. Apps	19
IX. City Passes, Tours, Best Views	20
X. Italian Phrases	22
XI. About Rome	25

I. General Info

GENERAL INFO

Facts & Info about Rome

Population: 4.2 million (2021)
Land area: 496 sq mi (1,285 km²)
Language: Italian (Romanesco dialect)
Best time to visit: April to June, mid-September to October to avoid summer heat and crowds
For how long: Min. 3-4 days
Currency: Euro (€ | EUR)

Covid-19 updates

Tourist info site

EU Visa: Schengen

Rome events

Drinking Water

Tap water is safe to drink. There are many free water fountains spread out across the city. Some fountains even offer sparkling water.

Toilets

There are only a few public toilets in Rome. Tip: go to a bar, order an espresso (1-2 EUR) and use the toilet. Or use a toilet in a museum.

I. General Info

Safety

Crime info

Rome is generally a safe destination, so you normally shouldn't be worried about specific areas to avoid or staying inside at night. Pay attention to pickpockets, especially around major attractions.

Emergency services number: 112
◂ **Crime rates**

Power Plugs

Type L
Type C

Italy uses the power plugs **type L** (Italy only) and **type C** (used in most of Europe). You can sometimes use plug type F (also used in most of Europe).

Travel Adapters

If you are coming from outside Italy or Europe, you will need a travel adapter to charge your phone & other devices.

Wheelchair access

Wheelchair

People with physical disabilities will encounter many challenges when visiting Rome, such as cobblestones and uneven ground, few accessible transportation options, hills, etc. Plan in advance.

◂ **Disabled Access Review**

MONEY

Currency

€ - Euro, used in most European Countries.

1 € is worth approximately:*

$ 1.13 USD
$ 1.44 CAD
$ 1.58 AUD
£ 0.84
¥ 131 JPY
₹ 84 INR
$ 23 MXN

Current rates

*Data for Jan. 2022

Credit Cards

Most hotels, shops, and restaurants in Rome accept major credit cards like Visa, MasterCard, or AMEX.

TIP: it is wise always to have some Euros in your wallet.

ATMs

There are plenty of ATMs in Rome. Use Google Maps or a similar app to find one.

III. Weather & Climate

WEATHER & CLIMATE

Rome has a Mediterranean climate with mild winters and hot and humid summers.

Spring

68 °F
20 °C
Average high

Weather in the spring is **unpredictable.**

43 °F - 73 °F
6 °C - 24 °C

Summer

86 °F
30 °C
Average high

Summers are **hot and humid** with little rain.

63 °F - 89 °F
17 °C - 31 °C

Fall

72 °F
22 °C
Average high

Fall is generally nice. It is still **warm and dry**.

45 °F - 81 °F
7 °C - 27 °C

Winter

55 °F
13 °C
Average high

Rain is common. Dec. which is the **wettest & most humid** month.

37 °F - 57 °F
3 °C - 14 °C

IV. Transportation

TRANSPORTATION

IV. Transportation - Fiumicino Airport

From and to FIUMICINO Airport (FCO)

Leonardo da Vinci Int. Airport is located approximately **19 miles** (30 km) from Rome's city center. You can use any of the following means of transportation:

- **Trains** ▾
  - Leonardo Express
  - Freccia (Trenitalia)
  - Regional (Trenitalia)
- **Bus:** Cotral, Terravision, etc.
- **Shuttle/transfer service**
- **Uber Office/Black/Van**
- **Taxi**
- **Car rentals**

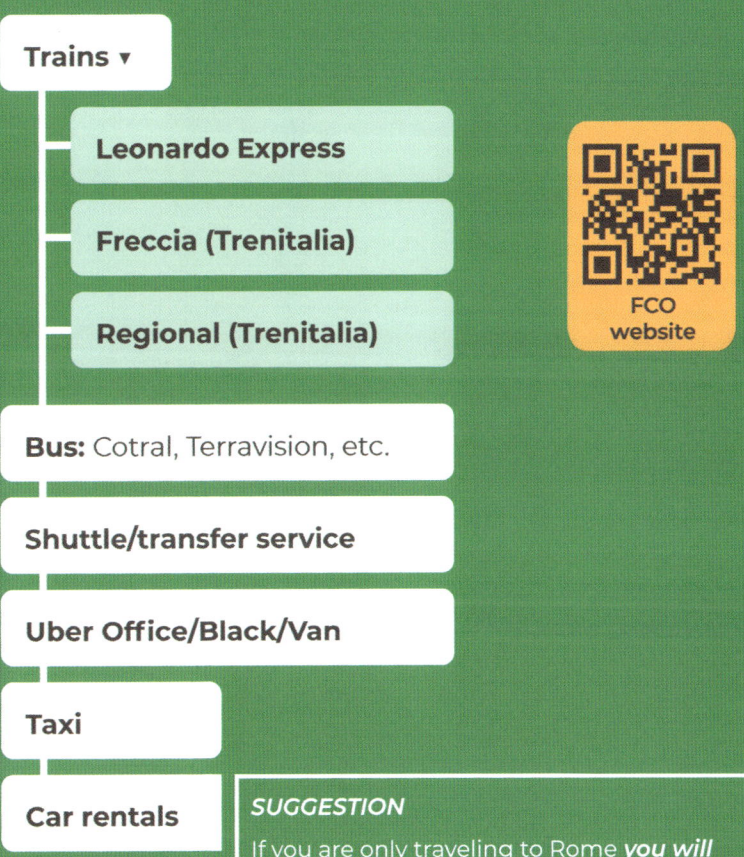

FCO website

SUGGESTION

If you are only traveling to Rome *you will probably not need a car*. Many hotels in Rome charge extra for car parking.

We recommend this option if you are also planning to drive to other parts of Italy.

IV. Transportation - Ciampino Airport

From and to CIAMPINO Airport (CIA)

Ciampino airport is located approximately **9 miles** (15 km) from Rome's city center. You can use any of the following means of transportation:

- **Regional Train**

  > **IMPORTANT!**
  > In order to use the train, you first have to take a 5-minute bus trip to Ciampino train station.

- **Bus**
- **Shuttle & transfer service**
- **Uber Black/Lux/Van**
- **Taxi**
- **Car rentals**

CIA website

SUGGESTION

If you are only traveling to Rome *you will probably not need a car* to drive around. Many hotels in Rome charge extra for car parking.

We only recommend this option if you are also planning to drive to other parts of Italy.

IV. Transportation - Train & Car

Arriving by TRAIN

You will normally arrive at Termini railway station, which is conveniently located in the Rome city center. You can check if your train also stops at one of the other major train stations in Rome.

- **Regular trains**
- **Le Frecce***
- **Italo****

Trains

*Including high-speed Frecciarossa connecting Turin-Milan-Bologna-Rome-Naples-Salerno
**Also a high-speed rail transport

Arriving by CAR

If you are arriving to Rome by car, consider renting a hotel or an apartment with a parking space or a garage nearby. Garages in the city center costs from **1-3 EUR per hour** and approximately **18 EUR per day** on average.

- **Garage:** Scan the QR code ▸
- **Park on the street:** 1-2 EUR/hour

Garages

IV. Transportation - Around the City

Getting AROUND THE CITY

While Rome is relatively well covered with public transportation, certain central areas are **at least about a 10-minute walk** away from the first underground station.

- **Walking**

  TIP: Walking will probably be part of your daily routine, so bring **comfortable shoes**

- **Public Transportation ▾**
  - Metro
  - Bus
  - Tram
  - Urban railway

  PRICES

One way *Valid for 75 min*	**1.5 EUR**
24h ticket	**7 EUR**
Weekly ticket	**24 EUR**

  You can buy tickets at tobacconists, bars, or vending machines at Metro stations and major bus stops.

- **Taxi/transfers**
- **Hop-on-hop-off Bus**
- **City bikes/bike rentals**
- **Vespa/car rentals**
- **Electric scooters**

Transp. options

IV. Transportation - Around the City

ACCOMMODATION

Average hotel price (2 people/night):

From 110 EUR
~ 130 USD

TIP 1: The price varies and depends on the location, facilities (level of luxury), weekdays vs. weekends, cancellation options, etc. Also, pay attention to extra charges like tourist tax, parking, breakfast, etc.

TIP 2: You can find better deals if you take the time to research multiple online booking platforms, like Airbnb or Booking. Also, be flexible with the dates when booking. Try to book accommodation with cancellation options.

To stay close to major attractions:
Stay between the Tiber river and Termini train station

If you don't mind spending a little more:
Stay close to Piazza Navona, Trevi Fountain, Piazza di Spagna, and Piazza Barberini

If you want to save some money:
Stay a little further away from the city center*

*Stay close to public transportation

VI: Food & Drinks

FOOD & DRINKS

We suggest using **Yelp** or **TripAdvisor** to find nearby places with good reviews. Try to avoid sitting down in the restaurants next to major attractions, many times you can find a much better price/quality ratio restaurants a street or two away from the main locations.

AVERAGE PRICES - bars, restaurants

DRINKS
Coffee	€ 1-2
Water	€ 1-2
Soda	€ 2-3
Aperol	€ 5-7
Wine	€ 2-6
Beer	€ 3-5

FOOD
Breakfast	€ 3-5
Avg. meal	€ 10-20
Pizza slice	€ 2-4
Pasta	€ 9-12
Ice-cream	€ 2-4

Cover charges (it. coperto) is illegal and cannot be charged in Rome. But service charge can be included.

Unique bars & eateries, best cheap eats

- Minerva Rooftop bar
- PanDivino
- Casina Valadier
- Pastificio Guerra

See map for more ▶

More here

GOOD TO KNOW

Lines & Crowds

Rome gets very crowded, especially in the summer and around major attractions. So be prepared to wait in line or buy a skip-the-line ticket or Rome City Pass.

Opening Hours

Restaurants, bars, and shops have different opening hours, and some of them are closed during a lunch break. Some restaurants are typically closed on Mondays and some even on Tuesdays.

Vacation in August

Some shops close in August as locals go on their vacation - Ferragosto or "Vacation in August" in Italian.

Internet: Wi-Fi, SIM, etc.

You can find WiFi metropolitano in the squares, parks, etc. You can purchase the prepaid SIM card to access internet or rent a pocket WiFi.

APPS

Restaurants, reviews

- **TripAdvisor**
- **Yelp**

Do things with locals

- **Eatwith** Eat with locals
- **Withlocals** Tours, etc.
- **Airbnb** Tours, etc.
- **Meetup** Group meetings

Other apps

- **Duolingo** Learn Italian
- **WiFi Map** Find WiFi
- **Viator** Book a tour
- **Google Translate**
- **Il Meteo** Weather app

Getting around

- **Google/Apple Maps**
- **Probus** Bus Routes
- **Moovit**
- **My Taxi**
- **Bird** El. scooters
- **Helbiz** Bikes
- **eCooltra** Scooters

Water & toilets

- **Flush**
- **I Nassoni**

Download apps

IX: City Passes, Tours, Best City Views

City Passes, Tours, Views

Rome City Pass

A great option to save money if you are planning to visit several museums and attractions and want to skip the line at some locations. You can even choose a city pass that combines attractions and public transportation.

Turbopass City Pass

Rome Pass

Omnia Card

Views - MAP

Best city views

- Altare della Patria
- St. Peter's Basilica
- Terrazza del Pincio
- Minerva Rooftop Bar
- Janiculum Terrace
- Terrazza Viale del Belvedere, etc.

◄ See map for more

IX: City Passes, Tours, Best City Views

City Tours

Walking tours of Rome are organized by professional tour guides who know a great deal about the city's rich history, legends, etc.

A great way to discover Rome. Some providers even offer free walking tours of the city, however, at the end of the tour it is recommended to give a donation of your choice to the tour guides.

- FREE and cheap guided tours
- Rome by Vespa Sidecar
- Pasta & Tiramisu Lovers Workshop
- Crypts & Roman Catacombs Tour
- Jewish Ghetto and Trastevere Tour
- Haunted Rome Ghost Tour
- Secrets of Rome Evening Tour
- Skip-the-Line: Vatican, Sistine Chapel
- Rome Segway Tour

Book your favourite tour

SOME ITALIAN PHRASES

Hello/bye
Ciao

Good morning, good day
Buongiorno
(formal: buona mattina)

Good afternoon
Buon pomeriggio

Good evening
Buonasera

Good night
Buona notte

Goodbye
Arrivederci

Welcome
Benvenuto

Please
Per favore

Thank you (many thanks/ thanks a lot)
Grazie (molto grazie/ grazie mille)

You're welcome
Prego

Sorry/excuse me
Mi scusi

Too much (that's too expensive!)
Troppo
(è troppo caro!)

A lot
Molto

A little
Poco

Yes
Sì

No
No

I don't speak italian.
Non parlo italiano.

Do you speak english?
Parla inglese?

I don't understand
Non capisco

Help!
Aiuto!

What's your name?
Come ti chiami?

My name is ____.
Mi chiamo, ___.

X: Italian Phrases

Dove? (Dov'è il museo?)
Where? (Where is the museum?)

Sugar
Zucchero

Starter
Antipasti

Primo
Main course

Salad
Insalata

Fish
Pesce

Rice
Riso

The bill, please
Il conto, per favore

Ice-cream
Gelato

I don't know.
Non lo so.

City
Città

Restaurant
Il ristorante

Store
Negozio

- DAYS OF THE WEEK -

Monday **Lunedi**	Friday **Venerdi**
Tuesday **Martedi**	Saturday **Sabato**
Wednesday **Miercoledi**	Sunday **Domenica**
Thursday **Giovedi**	

- NUMBES -

Zero **Zero**	Six **Sei**	Twenty **Venti**
One **Uno**	Seven **Sette**	Hundred **Cento**
Two **Due**	Eight **Otto**	Thousand **Mille**
Three **Tre**	Nine **Nove**	Million **Milione**
Four **Quattro**	Ten **Dieci**	
Five **Cinque**		

Learn Italian for free

ABOUT ROME

Rome is Italy's capital and, with a population of around three million, its largest city. Although Rome's official founding is estimated around 753 BC, the area was inhabited long before that. As a result, Rome's city center feels like one big open-air museum and is listed as a UNESCO World Heritage Site.

THE LEGEND OF ROMULUS AND REMUS

Rome was built on seven hills, and the legend says that it was founded by Romulus, who killed his twin brother Remus after the two of them have been raised by a she-wolf.

THE ROMAN EMPIRE

Following the Roman Republic's formation in 509 BC, Rome became the world's most dominant empire. With over one million inhabitants, the city also became the world's largest settlement.

THE CAPITAL OF ITALY

In 1870 Rome was chosen as the country's capital, following the unification of Italy, ending the Papal rule of the city. In 1971 Rome also became the seat of the king of Italy and remained the royal capital until 1946.

POPULAR TRAVEL DESTINATION

Rome is the most popular tourist destination in Italy and one of Europe's most visited cities. Around nine million tourists visit the Eternal city every year.

VATICAN CITY

Located within the city of Rome lies the world's smallest independent country, the seat of the Roman Catholic Church – Vatican City. Although formed long before that, the Vatican only became an independent country in 1911.

Section 2

Top 10 Things to Do in Rome

This section includes:

1. Roman Forum & Palatine Hill	29
2. Colosseum	33
3. Altare della Patria	35
4. Villa Borghese Gardens	37
5. Appia Antica Park & Catacombs	39
6. Trevi Fountain & Vicus Caprarius	43
7. Spanish Steps	47
8. Baths of Caracalla	49
9. Pantheon	51
10. Vatican City	53

Number 1a: Roman Forum & Palatine Hill

Buy tickets here

Number 1a: Roman Forum & Palatine Hill

Roman Forum

Center of public life in ancient Rome

1a

OPENING HOURS

9am-4:30pm
Daily

ENTRANCE FEE

18 EUR
Combined w/ Colosseum & Palatine

Location

Roman Forum was the **center of public life** in ancient Rome. Located next to the Colosseum and surrounded by government buildings and other important buildings, it was the venue of significant public events such as elections, criminal trials, processions, or public speeches.

After the fall of the Empire, the Forum was neglected. Later it was also used as a meadow for livestock and got its **nickname Cow Field** (it. Campo Vaccino). The site was first excavated in the 18th century. The area is now a big **open-air museum** featuring relatively well-preserved ruins of old buildings.

If you don't want to visit the museum, you can see a big part of the forum from the public street above.

i **Did you know?** The legend says that Romulus, the founder of Rome, is buried under the Roman Forum.

Number 1b: Roman Forum & Palatine Hill

Palatine Hill

A large open-air museum

Location

Rome is built on **seven hills**: Esquiline, Palatine, Aventine, Capitoline, Quirinal, Viminal, and Caelian Hill.

Located above Roman Forum, you will find the Palatine Hill.

According to a legend, the she-wolf that took care of **Romulus and Remus lived here**. The settlements on a Palatine Hill date back as far as 10th century BC. Today you can visit an impressive collection of archaeological sites from different eras of ancient Rome.

Don't skip the following attractions:

- **Domus Tiberiana:** first imperial Roman palace. Don't skip Neronian Cryptoporticus covered passageway
- **Flavian Palace:** public area built in 92 AD
- **House of Augustus:** primary home of the emperor Augustus
- **House of Livia**: mosaics, painted walls
- **Domus Flavia:** completed in 92 AD (a part of Palace of Domitian)
- **Stadio Palatino**, etc.

i **Did you know?** Palatine Hill is nicknamed "the first nucleus of the Roman Empire"

Number 1b: Roman Forum & Palatine Hill

Number 2: Colosseum

Number 2: Colosseum

Colosseum

The largest amphitheater ever built

OPENING HOURS

9am-4³⁰pm
Daily

ENTRANCE FEE

18 EUR
Combined w/
Roman Forum & Palatine

Location

Colosseum (Flavian Amphitheatre) is the **largest amphitheater ever built**. Construction of this remarkable structure was completed in the year 80. It was made using limestone, tuff, and concrete to demonstrate Roman building techniques to the entire world. Only 1/3 of the building is still visible today - earthquakes, fire, and vandalism damaged it over the years.

It was a gift from the people of Rome by the **Flavian Dynasty** to gain their popularity. The emperors organized events that were free to attend and sometimes even provided free food for the visitors. It could hold over 50,000 spectators. Colosseum was used for **gladiatorial combats,** animal hunts, executions, re-enactments of famous battles, a stage for performances, and other public spectacles.

i **Did you know?** The first-ever games held in 80 A.D. ran for 100 days straight.

Number 3: Altare della Patria

Number 3: Altare della Patria

Altare della Patria

Rome's largest monument

3

OPENING HOURS
9³⁰am-7³⁰pm
Daily

ENTRANCE FEE
Free

Location

Altar of the Fatherland or Altare della Patria is a large monument built on top of a part of Capitoline Hill. The monument was built **in honor of the first king** of unified Italy, Victor Emanuel II, and is the largest monument in Rome. The construction began in 1885, but the memorial was not completed for another 50 years, until 1935.

The construction of Il Vittoriano was controversial because destroyed a large part of the Capitoline Hill's Medieval neighborhood.

There you can visit the monument, a museum of Italian Unification, a tomb of the unknown soldier. Complete your tour by visiting its **impressive terrace** (free) with amazing views of Rome in all directions.

i **Tip:** get higher & visit the rooftop (tickets: 7 EUR)

Number 4: Villa Borghese Gardens

Bioparco di Roma (ZOO)

Number 4: Villa Borghese Gardens

Villa Borghese Gardens
Rome's Main Park

OPENING HOURS

24/7

ENTRANCE FEE

Free

Location

Villa Borghese is a **large public park** featuring numerous buildings, villas, museums, and other attractions. The park is located above Piazza Del Popolo, one of Rome's main squares.

The garden was **created in 1605** from a former vineyard. In the 19th century, the park was designed to its current form and was purchased by the city of Rome for public use.

Villa Borghese offers an array of activities: you can rent a boat on one of the lakes and row around the inspiring Temple of Asclepius, visit the **Waterclock** hydrochronometer at Pincio, a zoo (Bioparco di Roma), Borghese Museum, or stop at one of several open-air restaurants and cafes.

Don't skip **Terrazza del Pincio** that offers one of the best panoramic views of Rome.

i **Tip:** rent a boat on a scenic artificial lake

Number 5a: Appia Antica Park & Catacombs

Book a guided tour

Number 5a: Appia Antica Park & Catacombs

Appia Antica Park

Park featuring ancient ruins

5a

The Appia Antica Park or Appian Way Regional Park is an area located around about 10 miles (16 km) of the 2,300 year-old Via Appia road, starting in the center of Rome leading southeast.

Traveling along Via Appia, you can discover some of Rome's most remarkable **historical attractions**, some of which are still very well preserved.

You can almost feel like you are traveling back to ancient Roman times. Part of the road is still covered with the original, over **2,000 year-old stones**, surrounded by ruins of ancient villas, churches, and castles.

Location

Don't skip the following attractions: **Aqueduct Park** with ruins of ancient Roman aqueducts, Villa of the Quintilii, the Park of the Caffarella, the Tombs of Via Latina arc. zone, etc.

Number 5a: Appia Antica Park & Catacombs

5b

Book a guided tour

Number 5a: Appia Antica Park & Catacombs

Catacombs
...
Underground burial places

5b

MAP: Catacombs, tombs, crypts

Located along the Appia Antica Park, you will find several of the **Roman catacombs**. They are underground burial grounds mostly used for burying Christians and Jews from the 2nd to the 5th century AD.

While there are **over 60 catacombs in Rome**, with over 180 mi. or 300 km of underground passageways, only some of them are open to the public.

Visit catacombs:

- **Catacombs of San Sebastiano** (12 km long): former pozzolan mine was used as a place for pagan burial after the 2nd century. Later, the mausoleums were also used to bury Christians.
- **Catacombs of Domitilla** (12 km long): actively used as a Christian cemetery between 1st and 5th century with over 26,000 tombs
- **Catacombs of St. Callixtus:** half a million Christians were buried in this official cemetery in the 3rd century.

i **Did you know?** There are other catacombs in Rome like the Capuchin Crypt, Catacombs of Priscilla, etc.

Number 6b: Trevi Fountain & Vicus Caprarius

6a

Fountains MAP

Number 6b: Trevi Fountain & Vicus Caprarius

Trevi Fountain
...
One of the world's most famous fountains

6a

OPENING HOURS

24/7

ENTRANCE FEE

Free

Location

Trevi fountain was built on the façade of a palace in 1751, and it is one of the most famous fountains in the world. It stretches 86 feet (26 m) in the air and 161 feet (50 m).

The water for the fountain was delivered from **Acuqa Vergine**, one of Rome's aqueducts, and was considered to be the purest water one can drink in Rome (it is not safe to drink anymore).

The legend says that whoever drinks the water from the fountain or **throws a coin** in it will return to Rome.

There are over 2000 fountains in Rome. Discover some of the most impressive ones on the map (scan the QR code).

i **Did you know?** There is nearly 700,000 euros worth of coins are tossed into Trevi Fountain each year.

Number 6b: Trevi Fountain & Vicus Caprarius

Vicus Caprarius

Ancient Roman underground complex

Location

ENTRANCE FEE

4 EUR
8 EUR - Guided tour

OPENING HOURS

11am-5pm
Tue-Sun

Located below Trevi Fountain in the Trevi district, there is a **system of underground labyrinths** from the Roman Times, offering an insight into the life, engineering, and ingenuity of ancient Rome.

Discovered by chance during the construction of a local cinema in 1999, the so-called **Water City** or Vicus Caprarius is part of the complex Virgin Aqueduct that supplied potable water to the city, including the Trevi Fountain.

During excavation, a treasure trove with over 800 coins was discovered on site.

i **Did you know?** The Aqua Virgo was one of the 11 Roman aqueducts that was supplying the city with fresh water.

Number 6b: Trevi Fountain & Vicus Caprarius

Number 7: Spanish Steps

Number 7: Spanish Steps

Spanish Steps

Widest stairway in Europe

7

OPENING HOURS

24/7

ENTRANCE FEE

Free

Spanish Steps are a colossal stairway of 135 steps connecting the Spanish Embassy with the Trinità dei Monti church. The slightly elevated drainage system is often mistaken for the first step.

The steps were built in the **18th century** by a French diplomat Etienne Gueffier and took only two years to complete. As the widest stairway in Europe, Spanish Steps quickly gained recognition and eventually became one of the main Roman attractions.

At the bottom of the Spanish Steps, there is **Piazza di Spagna** with famous Fontana della Barcaccia, dating back to the early Baroque period.

i **Tip:** if you visit the Rome in May, part of the steps are decorated with pink Azaleas.

Number 8: Baths of Caracalla

Buy tickets here

Number 8: Baths of Caracalla

Baths of Caracalla

Center of daily life in ancient Rome

8

OPENING HOURS

9am-2/6³⁰pm
Depends on the day

ENTRANCE FEE

From **6 EUR**

Location

Bathing was a part of daily activities in Roman culture. Baths were the central part of Roman urban architecture. The impressive and vast complex of the Baths of Caracalla (now in ruins) was built between the year 212 and 216 by the Roman Emperor Caracalla to gain popularity.

People of different social classes came to the baths every day, not only to bathe but also to socialize. The Baths of Caracalla even featured an entire public library.

However, the baths also hide a darker side. In the **underground tunnels**, hundreds of slaves worked in extreme heat to keep the water warm all the time. The tunnels are now open to the public.

Visit **other ancient baths:** The Baths of Diocletian (the largest baths), Terme di Massenzio, Baths of Trajan, etc.

i **Don't miss:** Open air Teatro dell'Opera concerts

Number 9: Pantheon

Number 9: Pantheon

Pantheon

Best preserved ancient monument in Rome

OPENING HOURS

8:30/9am-5:45/7:15pm
Daily

ENTRANCE FEE

Free

Pantheon is a **former Roman temple**, constructed in the 2nd century AD by the Roman Emperor Hadrian. In 609, Pantheon was given to the pope and **converted into a church**.

Pantheon is the best-preserved ancient Roman monument. Its impressive concrete dome features an oculus in the center, which serves as the primary source of natural light.

Since there is **no glass covering the oculus** when it rains, the floor gets wet, but because of an ingenious system of 22 well-hidden holes, the water quickly drains away.

i **Don't miss:** The impressive oculus at the top of the dome, main source of natural light in Pantheon

Number 10: Vatican City

The Creation of Adam, Sistine Chapel

Vatican Museum Tickets

Number 10: Vatican City

Vatican City
...
World's smallest sovereign state

10

OPENING HOURS

24/7 Outside
Museums: vary
(scan the QR code)

ENTRANCE FEE

Free From outside
17+EUR Vatican Museums

Location

Covering an area of 110 acres (44 ha) and with only about 1,000 people, the Vatican City is the smallest state in the world by both area and population. The official name is Vatican City State and has been **the residence of the pope** since the year 1377.

While the central area is closed to the public, there are many attractions to see, for example, St. Peter's Square and Basilica are impressive examples of Renaissance architecture, or Vatican Gardens.

Visit **Vatican Museums**, displaying a collection of 20,000 works of art. Don't skip **Sistine Chapel** and one of the most famous frescos in the world *The Creation of Adam* (painted between 1508 and 1512) by Michelangelo.

i **Did you know?** The word Vatica or Vaticum means garden in Latin

Section 3

10 Additional Things to Do in Rome

This section includes:

11. Quartiere Coppedè	57
12. Circus Maximus	59
13. Piazza Navona	61
14. Gardens	63
15. Crypts & Mausoleums	67
16. Piazza del Popolo	69
17. Mouth of Truth	71
18. Ancient Walls & Gates	73
19. Roman Ghetto	75
20. Museums & Art Galleries	77

Number 11: Quartiere Coppedè

Number 11: Quartiere Coppedè

Quartiere Coppedè

Architectural fantasy quarter

OPENING HOURS
24/7

ENTRANCE FEE
Free

Location

Located in the Trieste district, you can discover a small but **unique quarter**, called Quartiere Coppedè.

The district is especially interesting because of its **mix of architectural styles**, from Art Noveau to medieval and Baroque buildings.

The quarter is similar to the architecture of Barcelona.

i **Don't miss:** The Fontana delle Rane (Frog Fountain) in the center of the street.

Number 12: Circus Maximus

Circo Maximo Experience

Number 12: Circus Maximus

Circus Maximus

Mass gathering venue in ancient Rome

12

OPENING HOURS
24/7

ENTRANCE FEE
Free

Location

Circus maximus is a **former chariot racing stadium** of ancient Rome. Circus Maximus was used for ludi (public games) connected to Roman religious festivals.

It was used as a mass entertainment venue and could host 150,000 people at once. Circus Maximus is 2,037 feet (621 m) long and 387 feet (118 m) wide. The archeological site is well preserved and you can experience it in its eternity.

For those who want to learn more, there is **a museum** you can visit, however, the stadium is clearly visible from all sites free of charge.

i **Don't miss:** Circo Maximo Experience - a history through augmented and virtual reality

Number 13: Piazza Navona

Circus Agonalis

Number 13: Piazza Navona

Piazza Navona
...
Former Dominitian's stadium

13

OPENING HOURS

24/7

ENTRANCE FEE

Free

Location

Piazza Navona is a Baroque square from the late 15th century that features several impressive statues and fountains from Baroque architecture.

The square was built in the 1st century on a **former Dominitian's stadium**. The stadium was used for the athletics competitions (Latin: agones games) and was known as "Circus Agonalis" or the competition arena. You can still recognize the square's unique shape and visit the ruins of the stadium 4.5 metres (15 ft.) under Piazza Navona (Unesco World Heritage Site). Later in history, the square became a lake during the summer to stage naval battles.

There are **legends about ghosts** (Donna Olimpia & Costanza de Cupis) who wonder around the square.

i **Did you know?** Fontana dei Quattro Fiumi was featured in Dan Brown's thriller Angels and Demons.

Number 14a: Gardens

Number 14a: Gardens

Giardino Del Teatro

...

One of many amazing gardens in Rome

OPENING HOURS

24/7

ENTRANCE FEE

Free

Location

Rome is home to several impressive gardens. One of the best examples is Giardino Del Teatro with 184 hectares built in the Pamphili estate in the mid-17th century.

It houses **impressive buildings** and other architectural elements and is a popular spot for locals to jog.

Some of the **main attractions** include Villa Doria Pamphili, Pamphili Chapel, Belvedere Lake with Fontana del Giglio, catacombs of San Pancrazio, etc. The garden looks like it was lost in time.

i **Tip:** walk around the gardens and admire its many fountains, abandoned statues and buildings

Number 14b: Gardens

14b

Other gardens
. . .
Impressive green areas

Rome Rose Garden

It is a public rose park established in 1931 located near the Roman Ghetto (former Jewish cemetery). Don't skip the nearby **Giardino degli Aranci** (▲ photo above) with panoramic city views.

Villa Ada Savoia

One of the largest parks in Rome from the 17th century with many hiking paths, bike rentals, café, live music festivals. Don't skip a former royal bunker, a small lake, Temple of Flora, etc.

Parco Villa Celimontana

It is a park around Villa Celimontana that sits on the Caelian Hill (one of seven ancient hills). It also contains some Roman ruins.

Number 14b: Gardens

The Aventine Keyhole

All parks MAP

Number 15: Crypts & Mausoleums

St. Angelo Bridge and Castel Sant'Angelo Castle

Number 15: Crypts & Mausoleums

Crypts & Mausoleums

Extravagant burial grounds of Roman dignitaries

MAP: Catacombs, tombs, crypts

During its rich and diverse history, Romans were always exploring for new places to bury their dignitaries. As a result, Rome is full of mausoleums, crypts, and catacombs, many of them underground:

- **Pyramid of Cestius**: is an ancient pyramid built around 18–12 BC & a tomb for Gaius Cestius, a member of the Epulones religious corporation.

- **Castle Sant'Angelo:** Hadrian Mausoleum, later used by popes and as a fortress and a castle. The building is now an impressive museum.

- **The Capuchin Crypt:** located beneath the church of Santa Maria della Concezione dei Cappuccini. It contains the remains of 3,700 bodies, believed to be the Capuchins.

- **Mausoleum of Augustus:** it is a large tomb built in 28 BC by the Roman Emperor Augustus

Other tombs:

- Tomb of the Scipios
- Tomb of Eurysaces the Baker, etc.

Number 16: Piazza del Popolo

Number 16: Piazza del Popolo

Piazza del Popolo

Once a first sight upon entering Rome

16

OPENING HOURS

24/7

ENTRANCE FEE

Free

Location

Located under Villa Borghese gardens, you will find Piazza del Popolo, which translates to People's Square. But the actual name comes from the word *populous* – a Latin name for a type of tree that is believed to have been growing there.

It is one of the largest open areas in the historic city center and was the location of public executions; the latest one was carried out in 1826.

Piazza del Popolo is located on the inside of the **Porta del Popolo**, the gates to Rome, and was the first thing travelers would see when entering Rome.

The square features an impressive **Egyptian obelisk** of Ramesses II, which was transported to Rome in 10 BC.

i **Don't miss:** Terrazza del Pincio above the square with panoramic views of Piazza del Popolo

Number 17: Mouth of Truth

Number 17: Mouth of Truth

Mouth of Truth

A mysterious Roman legend

OPENING HOURS

9:30am-5:50pm

Daily

ENTRANCE FEE

2 EUR

Free from outside

Location

Bocca Della Verità or The Mouth of Truth is a famous marble mask located in the portico of the Cosmedin Church in Rome. It is believed to depict the face of the **sea god Oceanus**.

While historians are not certain about the origin, and purpose of the disc, according to the legend, if you lie when placing your hand inside the mask, **the mouth will cut your hand**. You can visit the Mouth of Truth, tell a lie, and see for yourself if the legend is true. Mouth of Truth became famous after apearing in 1953 movie "Roman Holiday"

Don't skip the fountain and the two ancient roman temples: Temple of Hercules Victor Tempio di Portuno across the street.

i **Tip:** visit the nearby Tiber Island. It was once used as a hospital as well as a temple. The island is commonly linked to medicine and healing.

Number 18: Ancient Walls & Gates

Number 18: Ancient Walls & Gates

Ancient Walls & Gates

Two separate systems of walls with gates

MAP: Ancient Gates

The Romans built walls and gates **to protect from the invaders** and impress the travelers arriving in the city.

During ancient times, there were two separate systems of walls, constructed each in their respective era.

The Servian Wall was built in 4th century BC and was 6.8 mi. (11 km) long built of volcanic tuff. The wall was named after the sixth Roman King, Servius Tullius and is believed to have 16 main gates (none survived).

The Aurelian Walls was constructed in 271 AD and was 12 miles (19 km). The construction of the wall was a reaction to the city's vulnerability (after the barbarian invasion of 270). Parts of the walls are still visible throughout Rome together with several gates.

There were more walls built later on: Leonine wall & Janiculum wall.

i **Did you know?** The gates were closed after dusk and were under watch during the day to keep control of people entering and leaving Rome.

Number 19: Roman Ghetto

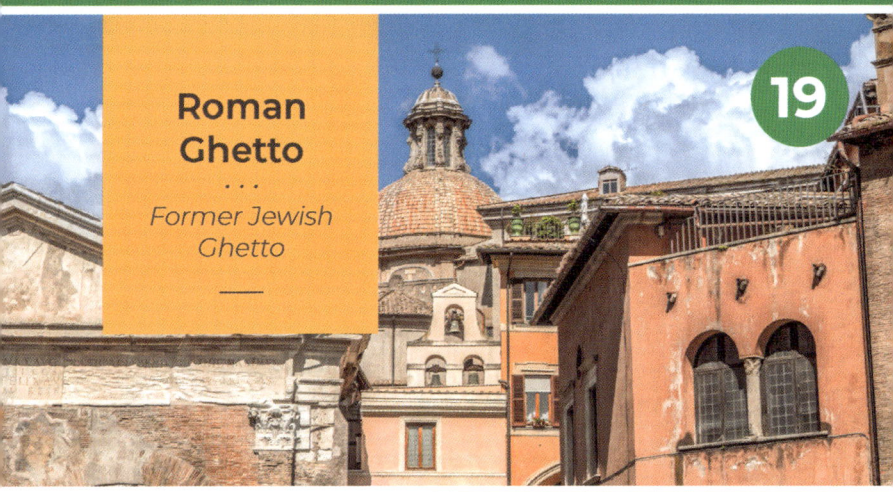

Roman Ghetto

Former Jewish Ghetto

Roman Ghetto was a **Jewish ghetto** from 1555 close to the River Tiber. It was controlled by the papacy until 1870. It is supposed to be the oldest in the world outside of the Middle East.

The first record of Jews in Rome dates back to 161 BC. The papal bull (public decree) required the Jews to live in the walled ghetto that was situated in undesirable quarters of the city with the Tiber river constantly flooding. Around 3,500 jews lived there under **inhuman conditions**. During the 1656 epidemic, 800 jews died.

They also faced many restrictions, including the prohibition of property ownership or practicing medicine. They had to wear yellow cloth (men) or a yellow veil (women) when they went outside the ghetto.

The ghetto walls were torn down in 1888. Because they were isolated for hundreds of years, they **developed their own dialect**, known as Giudeo-romanesco.

i **Tip:** visit Jewish museum & Great Synagogue of Rome

Number 20: Museum & Art Galleries

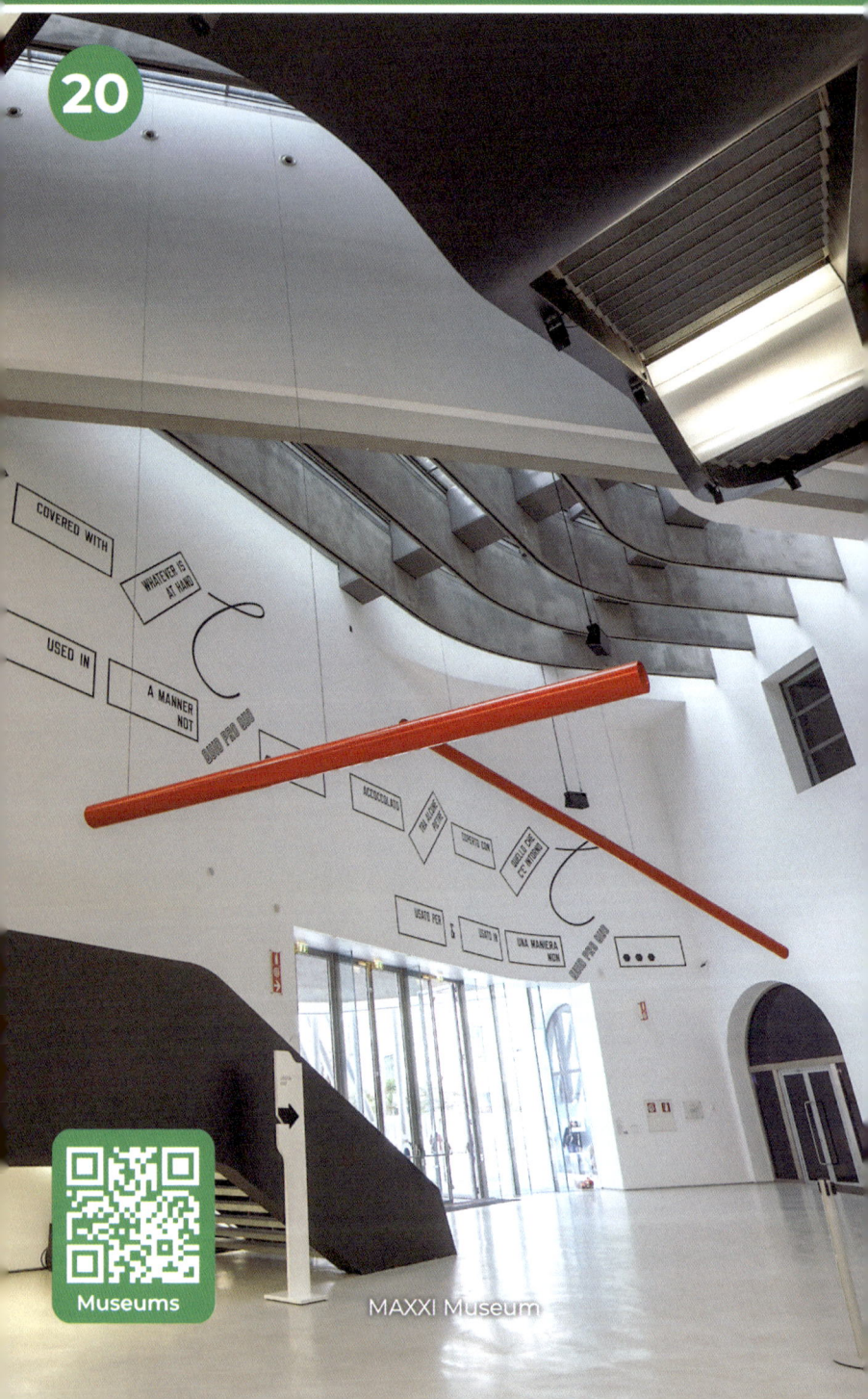

MAXXI Museum

Number 20: Museum & Art Galleries

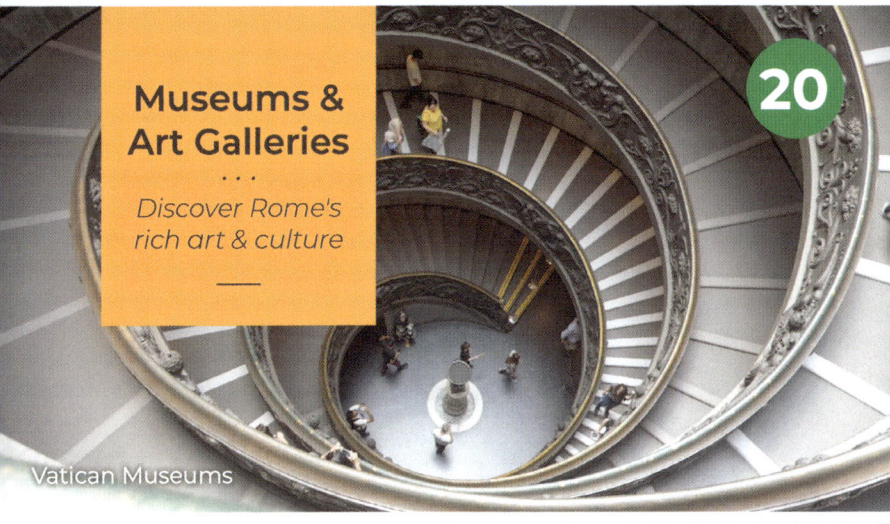

Museums & Art Galleries
...
Discover Rome's rich art & culture

Vatican Museums

Location

Rome is home to numerous impressive museums and art galleries:

- **Maxxi:** national museum of contemporary art and architecture
- **Capitoline Museums:** a group of art and archaeological museums on top of Capitoline Hill
- **Galleria Borghese:** an art gallery
- **Museums of walls:** an archaeological museum
- **La Galleria Nazionale:** an art gallery
- **Museum of Rome:** art museum founded in the Fascist era
- **Doria Pamphili Gallery:** art collection
- **Palazzo Massimo alle Terme:** Archaeological museum, etc.

Interesting museums:

- ViGaMus: interactive video game museum
- Metropoliz Museum of the Other and the Elsewhere in a former salami factory
- Museum of the Souls of Purgatory

Section 4

Itineraries, Things to Do, Best Day Trips

This section includes:

1. One Day Itinerary	80
2. Two Day Itinerary	81
3. Three Day Itinerary	82
4. Best Day Trips	84
5. Things to do...	85

1. One Day Itinerary

ITINERARIES

To make your trip to Rome stress-free and organized, we prepared simple one, two, and three-day itineraries. Each suggested itinerary includes a dedicated link to a customized Google Map that you can easily use on your phone.

 ◀ MAP

1-Day Itinerary

Morning

- Colosseum
- Admire Roman forum from the street above OR if time: Roman forum and Capitoline Hill
- Altare della Patria: terace with a beautiful city views
- Pantheon

Afternoon

- Galleria Sciarra
- Trevi Fountain
- Spanish Steps
- Terrazza Viale del Belvedere
- Villa Borghese
- Piazza del Popolo
- If time: Saint Peter's Square - Vatican

Evening

Explore Trastevere

2-Day Itinerary

MAP ▶

Day 1

Morning

- Colosseum
- Roman forum and Capitoline Hill
- Altare della Patria
- Marcello Theater from outside
- Tiber Island/Mouth of Truth - if time

Afternoon

- Roman Ghetto
- Campo de' Fiori
- Piazza Navona
- Pantheon
- Galleria Sciarra
- Fontana di Trevi
- Spanish Steps
- Villa Borghese
- Piazza del Popolo
- Vatican City

Evening

Go to a jazz club

Day 2

Morning

Via Appia Antica: catacombs, Appia ancient road, Parco degli Acquedotti, etc.

Afternoon & Evening

- Cestius Pyramid & Porta San Paolo
- Baths of Caracalla
- Circo Massimo - if time
- Rome Rose Garden - if time
- Orange Gardens (for the sunset)

Evening

- Embark on a wine/food tour
- Explore Trastevere
- Sip a glass of wine in one of many bar terraces

3. Three Day Itinerary

 ◂ MAP

3-Day Itinerary

Day 1

Morning
- Colosseum
- Roman forum and Capitoline Hill
- Altare della Patria

Afternoon & Evening
- Galleria Sciarra
- Fontana di Trevi
- Trevi Fountain
- Spanish Steps
- Terrazza Viale del Belvedere, Viale del Belvedere
- Villa Borghese
- Piazza del Popolo
- Embark on a wine or food tour

Day 2

Morning
Vatican City: the square, basilica, museums

Day 2 - continue

Afternoon & Evening
- Castel Sant'Angelo
- Piazza Navona
- Pantheon
- Campo de' Fiori
- Roman Ghetto
- Tiber Island - if time
- Mouth of Truth
- Orange Gardens - for the sunset

Day 3

Morning
- Circus Maximus - if time
- Baths of Caracalla
- Cestius Pyramid & Porta San Paolo

Afternoon & Evening
- Via Appia Antica
- Explore Trastevere

Day Trips From Rome

Villa d'Este (Tivoli)

16th-century villa with terraced hillside is now a museum and listed as a UNESCO World Heritage Site.

Civita di Bagnoregio

Founded over 2,500 years ago, this town is located on top of a plateau and is in constant danger of erosion.

Parco Ostia Antica

It is a large archeological park and is believed to be Rome's first colony. Ostia was Rome's main port because of its location (Tiber river outflow).

Royal Palace of Caserta

Palace (UNESCO World Heritage Site) is the largest royal residence in the world in terms of volume. Don't skip over 3 km long garden with fountains and pools.

Amalfi, Napoli, Pompeii & Vesuvius

Amalfi is a picturesque Italian coastline with charming little towns, wrapped between the sea and high hills. Pompeii were buried under volcanic ash in the eruption of Mount Vesuvius. Don't skip Napoli - city rich in history & cuisine.

5. Things to do...

Activities & links

Things to do...

...IN THE SUMMER

- Attend summer festivals, concerts & other events:
- Outdoor cinemas like Caleidoscopio
- Chill in one of many rooftop bars
- Go for an ice cream
- Explore parks and gardens
- Summer Music Festival at Terme di Caracalla
- Visit museums
- Visit underground attractions, like catacombs
- Take a boat ride on Tiber river
- Seagway tour
- Urban rafting on Tiber river

...IN THE WINTER

- Try ice skating, like the rings at Galleria Porta di Roma, Christmas Wonderland, Auditorium Parco della Musica, etc.
- Attend Christmas markets in December, like the one at Piazza Navona, Piazza di Spagna, etc.
- Attend cooking or baking classes
- Visit museums
- Go shopping: Galleria Alberto Sordi, Campo de' Fiori, Shopping Mall Porta di Roma, Rinascente Roma Tritone, etc.

Things to do...

...IF IT'S RAINING

- Visit underground attractions like: The catacombs, Vicus Caprarius, Domitian Stadium remains under Piazzan Navona, etc.
- Visit covered markets: Mercato di Testaccio, Campagna Amica Market,...
- Attend a cooking class
- Visit museums, art galleries, etc.
- Go to a bar or coffee shop
- Go shopping: Galleria Alberto Sordi, Shopping Mall Porta di Roma, Rinascente Roma Tritone, etc.

...IN THE EVENING

- Embark on a night walking tour to learn about ghosts and legends of Rome
- Go to one of many unique bars
- Attend a show, a concert, opera, etc.
- Cinema under the stars (in the summer): Caleidoscopio (Casa del Cinema), Il Cinema in Piazza, etc.
- Explore Trastevere
- Listen to some jazz
- Embark on a food or wine tour
- Attend a football game

5. Things to do...

Activities & links

- Rome Travel Guide by Hungry Passport
4225 Solano Ave. Ste 463, Napa CA 94558, USA

www.hungrypassport.xyz

© 2022 Hungry Passport Media Inc.

All rights reserved. No portion of this book may be reproduced in any form without permission from the publisher, except as permitted by U.S. copyright law. For permissions contact:

support@hungrypassport.xyz

CREDITS: Cover photo: Adobe Stock | P2: Hungry Passport Travel Guide page exports, Envato (scanning QR code, mobile phone), Google Maps PrtScn | P4: Adobe Stock| P6 (from above): Envato, Envato, Tim Mossholder/Pexels | P7: 123rf (power plugs & outlet styles) | P8 (from above): Envato, Envato, Envato | P9: Envato (weather icons) | P10: Twenty20 | P15: Adobe Stock | P17: Envato | P18 (from above): Twenty20, Envato, Envato | P20: Envato | P24: Adobe Stock | P28: Adobe Stock | P29: Envato | P30: Adobe Stock | P31: Adobe Stock | P32: Adobe Stock | P33: Envato | P34: Adobe Stock | P35: Adobe Stock | P36: Adobe Stock | P37: Adobe Stock | P38: Adobe Stock | P39: Adobe Stock (top), Adobe Stock (bottom) | P40: Adobe Stock | P41: Adobe Stock | P42: Envato | P43: Adobe Stock | P44: Hungry Passport | P45: Nick Bondarev/Pexels | P46: Adobe Stock | P47: Adobe Stock | P48: Adobe Stock | P49: Adobe Stock | P50: Adobe Stock | P51: Adobe Stock | P52: Adobe Stock | P53: Adobe Stock | P56: Adobe Stock | P57: Adobe Stock (top), Adobe Stock (bottom) | P58: Adobe Stock | P59: Adobe Stock | P60: Adobe Stock | P61: Adobe Stock | P62: Hungry Passport | P63: Adobe Stock (top), Hungry Passport (bottom) | P64 (from above): Adobe Stock, Adobe Stock, Adobe Stock, Adobe Stock | P65: Adobe Stock | P66: Hungry Passport | P67: Adobe Stock | P68: Hungry Passport | P69: Adobe Stock | P70: Adobe Stock | P71: Adobe Stock | P72: Adobe Stock | P73: Adobe Stock | P74: Adobe Stock | P75: Adobe Stock | P76: Adobe Stock | P77: Millie Greaves/Unsplash | P84: Adobe Stock | P85: Adobe Stock (icons) | P86: Adobe Stock (icons) | P87: Adobe Stock | Icons throughout this guide: Envato & Hungry Passport | Back cover: Hungry Passport Travel Guide mockup, Envato (scanning QR code)

Written & Designed by Hungry Passport © All Rights Reserved

Printed in Great Britain
by Amazon

84422088R00051